There's an Elephant in the Room

Discover the Single Most Powerful
Tool for Growth

OTHER LEADERSHIP BOOKS
BY MATT RAWLINS

The Green Bench
A dialogue about leadership and change

The Green Bench II
Ongoing Dialogue about Leadership
and Communication

The Lottery
A question can change a life

There's an Elephant in the Room

Discover the Single Most Powerful Tool for Growth

Matt Rawlins Ph.D.

Amuzement Publications

(The company and characters in this story are fictional)

Elephant Art by Ron Rieman

There's an Elephant in the Room by Matt Rawlins. Copyright © 2008 Matt Rawlins. All rights reserved. No part of this publication may be reproduced, stored in a retrieval system, or transmitted in any form or by any means -- electronic, mechanical, photocopy, recording, or any other -- except for brief quotations in printed reviews, without the prior permission of the publisher.

ISBN 1-928715-09-5

Dedication

This book is dedicated to my friends in Singapore. Thank you Syd, Jaz, Simon, Wee San, Andrew, Bee Leem, Leonard, Buzzi, Jim, CeCe, Kin Yun, Heriet, Wendy, Kevin, Jenny and Greg for your friendship. Without you it wouldn't have been possible to write.

A special thanks to Jaz who is a brilliant editor. You helped bring this to life.

Also a special thanks to my friend Ron Rieman who is an excellent artist. He drew the elephants. He has volunteered the last 16 years of his life to teaching students to become artists in Cambodia.

There's an Elephant in the Room

Contents

Day One 10

Day Two 27

Day Three 38

Day Four 49

Day Five 55

Day Six 65

Day Seven 81

Day Eight 108

Epilogue 113

Appendix A- Dealing with Elephants..... 116

Author's note 118

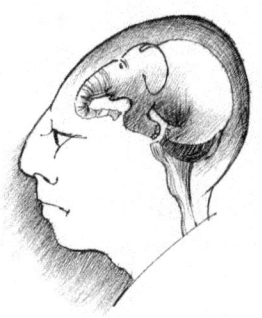

Houltren Manufacturing is an old and well-known company in our city. It is common knowledge that it was also very 'tired' with some even saying it was dying. People were leaving and there were accusations of bad management.

But in the last two years it had somehow managed amazing growth and as a result, has been on all the news programs. It has even been the subject of a case study at one of the largest universities in the US. When we are asked, this is the story we tell.

• • •

It took the older man an hour to find the room. He had never fully realized how big the company building was. It had been a long time since he had been to this corner of the building and a sinking realization was growing with each step. Finally, coming to the end of a long musty corridor, he stood at last in front of the door marked Room 423 and sensed that it was the beginning of the end of his career.

While standing there fidgeting with his glasses in front of the door, he heard someone walking down the hallway towards him. He turned to look and saw a young man wearing a bemused expression and a shirt a size too tight strolling slowly towards him. The older man pointed to the door number and said, "Room 423, Change Committee?"

The young man looked relieved to see another person; he said to the older man, "Hey, I'm Andrew from Human Resource."

The older man replied, "Hi, Andrew. I'm Simon from Production. Looks like we meet in here." With that, Simon opened the door and switched on the light as he walked in. Andrew followed behind him. It was a small room with only one window looking out at the side of the brick building next to them.

They closed the door and then walked over to the chairs around the small conference table in the middle of the room. They sat down slowly, looked around the room and didn't say anything. Finally Simon said rather crisply, "Let's wait for a couple more people before we start." He wasn't feeling at all sure of himself but felt he had to 'take charge' of the situation.

Andrew sat staring rather glumly at the room and nodded his head. He was already feeling like this meeting would be a waste of his time. But just then a small Asian woman appeared as the door opened. Simon and Andrew stood to greet her. She walked over to Andrew and Simon and introduced herself, "I'm Bee Lim from Finance." Immediately, Bee Lim wondered if the young man was sizing her up while the older man smiled at her rather patronizingly. After the introductions, just as they were sitting down, the door opened (again) and a young woman in jeans and a t-shirt strolled in. She had tattoos on her arm and a pierced eye-brow. She walked over and shook hands but strangely pointed at her name badge instead of saying anything.

Simon looked at her name tag and said, "Hi Buzzi from… the art department (actually, he hadn't heard of the art department but he wasn't about to let it show)." He looked closer and read out the small print under her name: "I can't talk, but I can hear, so please don't talk louder at me."

Simon asked with some uncertainty (but not as much as he actually felt), "I'm sorry, do you have laryngitis?"

Buzzi gave him a sad look and then bent over the pad of paper she carried with her. She took out her pencil, and wrote on the pad briefly and then held it up to Simon. He read her words out loud for the group, *'I was born without a voice box.'*

Simon looked away from her quickly with a brief apology, "Oh, I'm sorry." He turned to sit, trying to hide his confusion. Buzzi sat down and wrote out on her pad, *'I'm not'*, and then held it up to the group. Simon looked at it and said, "You're not?" with a mixture of shock and disbelief on his face.

Buzzi looked Simon straight in the eyes and then pointed to her throat. Simon still had a question on his face but Buzzi pointed again to the first words she wrote.

"Oh, you're not sorry about being born without a voice box. Okay then, well," he looked to Andrew and Bee Lim for support but found none and so he continued, "Here we are. As you all might know, it is rumored that each one of us has been carefully selected (he said this with some emphasis) by the Robinsons; they are the family that owns the majority share of this company. We do know the executive managment has offered us this prestigious (at the mention of this word he raised his voice slightly) job of overseeing the changes going on in the company this year."

Bee Lim sat and smiled awkwardly while Andrew sat looking out the window. Buzzi held her pad of paper in her lap and was drawing on it. By now Simon refused to even look at Buzzi and continued, "You may not know this but our company reports suggest that we are not doing very well. We have been losing market share for a while now and our quality and customer service have been rather, well, let's just say, there is room for growth. So, we were selected to try to bring about some changes in our company. Blah, Blah, Blah… *(It was being piled on thick and steady and there is no need to bother you with all that Simon was saying.)*."

After about 10 minutes of talking at them, Simon summoned the courage to look over at Buzzi who had stopped drawing and was looking up. She had a contagious smile on her face that totally disarmed him.

Buzzi motioned at the drawing she had made and seemed to want to show it to the group. Simon reluctantly said, "Yes, okay, show us what you have drawn."

Buzzi tore the paper off the pad and slid it onto the table.

Simon stared at it and was speechless. Andrew looked at Bee Lim who had a shocked look on her face as she looked away quickly. Before Andrew could get his hand over his mouth, he broke out and started laughing out loud. Bee Lim had her hand over her mouth struggling to keep a straight face but soon she also started to chuckle. Then Andrew looked at Simon and said, "She nailed you, dude. She just summed up everything you just said to us."

Simon looked over at Buzzi who again smiled with an amazingly disarming smile and then she wrote out, *'I can't speak, but I can hear very well. That is all that I heard.'*

Simon looked again at the picture of crap on the table. He looked over at Andrew who was still laughing, Bee Lim who was trying to hide her chuckle, and then back to Buzzi who had that contagious smile on her face with her eyes wide open. He fidgeted with his glasses and slowly a smile found its way onto Simon's face, then it grew, and finally he began to laugh too.

With great relief they all laughed long and hard *(If we had only known each other better then, we might have understood that it was the first time some of us had laughed hard in years)*.

As the laughter slowly eased up, Andrew pulled the picture over to himself, "May I borrow your pencil, Buzzi?" Buzzi handed the pencil over to Andrew like she was giving him her sword. He took it and wrote on the bottom of the image and then turned it around for all to see,

The Crap Stops Here

Simon looked at the drawing and smiled to himself. He looked up at the group and declared, "Okay, my new friends. This is our unofficial slogan for the group. Thank you, Buzzi, for the work of art and Andrew for the mission statement." With a smirk on his face, he added, "On behalf of upper management, I am glad to have modeled how our company works. We seem to have developed and refined the art of talking a lot of crap."

They smiled at each other and sat in silence for a moment. Buzzi bent over and started to draw quickly on her pad. Simon, Andrew and Bee Lim looked at each other and shrugged with a questioning look on their faces. Finally Simon stated the obvious, "I guess Buzzi has something to say. Whenever you are ready."

Buzzi looked up and nodded and went back to work. .

Simon said, "You have us all on pins and needles. Please show us your idea."

Buzzi tore the page off the pad and slid it onto the table.

An Elephant in the Room

Andrew asked out loud, "Is that the source of the ... er... crap?"

Buzzi smiled and pointed over at Simon while she shook her head.

Andrew declared, "Dude, she is pointing at you."

Simon said, "I can see that, thank you Andrew. I think what Buzzi just said was that I represent the source of the problem and... I have already agreed with that. I think maybe Buzzi is very perceptive, scarily so, I might add, and can see exactly what the problem is."

Buzzi smiled and nodded her head.

Simon continued, "Okay, as the old saying goes, there is an elephant in the room. It is a metaphor for some aspect of life that we are all aware of but can't talk about."

Bee Lim offered, "In Asia there are still some groups of people that work with elephants. The elephant is a symbol of strength."

Andrew added, "An elephant is also a symbol of strength in a room, just that no one knows how to deal with it. We don't get much elephant training here."

Simon gave a quick glance at Andrew, as if to note that Andrew's brashness hid a certain sharpness of mind and agreed, saying, "Yes, it is something strong or major that is on everyone's mind, impossible to ignore – like an elephant in a room. But nobody talks about the 'elephant' because no one knows what to do about it. It is the "secret" everyone knows."

Bee Lim smiled, "I get it: big, very present in a room, and felt by all. But no one wants to 'lose face' so you pretend it is not there."

Buzzi sat nodding her head at the comments being made.

Simon stayed quiet for a while and then, with a deep breath, he said in a firm voice, "Yes, that is the essence of it. Okay, let me start over. It seems we got off to a 'normal' start... for our company culture, that is. I am afraid I have been in management too many years and it seems to come naturally. I don't say what I mean or even mean what I say. So let me begin again with our new mission statement in mind." And then, like a dam that had been holding back a torrent, being released, Simon began to speak thoughts he hadn't recognized in a long time,

"It seems only a few people want to change.

Most of us are trying desperately to just be comfortable in our secure little pigeonholes.

However, the life of almost everyone who works here is slowly being squeezed out of them and few will admit it.

The company is slowly dying.

They picked us because we can easily become scapegoats if we make too much trouble and I think they are pretty sure we will do nothing and so they feel safe."

Andrew, Bee Lim and Buzzi sat and stared at Simon for a moment with a look of shock on their faces. Simon looked back at them somewhat pleased at the effect of his words, "What? You said the crap stopped here. I was just trying to honor our mission statement."

"Whoa, dude, take a breath. You just sucked all the air out of the room. We said, be honest, but let's ease into it," Andrew said ruefully. He hadn't expected anything much to happen at this meeting.

Buzzi shot Andrew a look that almost knocked him off his chair. She then looked at Simon and stood and clapped. Bee Lim gave an awkward look at Buzzi standing and Andrew sitting there, and finally stood and clapped too, saying, "I am with Buzzi. Thank you, Simon. I am so tired of all the words flying around here that mean nothing, I am ready to leave."

Buzzi turned and faced Bee Lim and applauded her this time.

Andrew stood up slowly and said rather belligerently, "You want honesty? My wife just walked out on me. She says she has had enough. She wants change or else it's over!"

Buzzi turned to face Andrew with a bewildered look for a moment and then nodded vigorously in approval. Simon said nervously, "I have a daughter who won't talk with me. I think she hates me."

Buzzi leaned down and sketched a quick picture. When she was done, she turned it around.

She motioned to herself and wrote the words, '*Painful, Lonely*' at the bottom of the page.

Bee Lim looked at Buzzi and said, "I understand your picture. That is also me, as an Asian woman growing up with my Western friends."

The honesty was unsettling, but we spent the next hour talking about life and the areas we suddenly found the courage to bring up. We learned more about each other in that short time than anyone else in the company ever had.

Simon finally called the meeting to order, for he still felt that he was in "in-charge", "Okay team, it doesn't seem like anything we did this morning has had anything to do with change, but I must admit that it has been a breath of fresh air. I am sure they will ask for some kind of an action plan, so please start thinking about what we need to do to begin a change program."

"The others all nodded in agreement recognizing that the committee needed to show some reportable action. They all got up to leave and walked out with another meeting planned for the next day. Simon joked as he opened the door, "I guess we don't have to worry about someone else taking our space. We can leave what we need here." They all chuckled and walked out.

Little did we know it, but in a small corner meeting room in a forgotten part of a dying company, life broke out. It wasn't meant to be that way, but life has a way of showing up at the most unusual places.

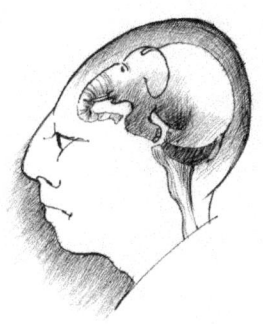

DAY TWO

Simon was late for work the next day. He rushed through the large foyer and down the hall towards Production. He turned towards his office and there on his office door was the picture of the elephant from the Change Committee meeting the night before. He was shocked at first and then smiled. He looked at his secretary and asked slyly, "What's that?"

His secretary replied, "It was there when I came in, Simon. I don't know how it got there. I left it as I thought it might be some kind of a bad joke you would want to see personally to deal with. It is signed by the Change Committee."

Simon smiled, "Yes, thank you. I am not sure how it got there but I do have my ideas." He walked into his office and just because he could, he left the picture of the elephant there.

Each of the other members of the Change Committee found the same picture posted on his or her own door. As more people caught sight of the curious picture, there was a lot of whispering about the elephant and what it meant. Still, no one talked about it out loud or at meetings, but then again, that was reality in a dying company.

• • •

They all quickly sat down in their obscure meeting room. Simon fiddled with his glasses and began, "Okay, we have not agreed on any action and we still have to get approval for any work from one of the company directors."

Andrew slid the picture of crap out on the table and coughed out his message as if it were a secret being passed to someone, "Sounds like a load of crap." He smiled and looked at Bee Lim and Buzzi who smiled back at him. Then he stated more clearly (and slightly smugly), "It seems one day away from us and you are already acting like one of 'them' again."

Simon took a deep breath and chuckled apologetically, "Thank you Andrew, I do need the reminder. Since we have agreed on no elephants in our meetings, I guess I should ask this. Who put up the signs?"

Andrew hesitantly raised his hand, "I did. I came back later and made copies of the elephant and put it up on our doors. I figured we might need the reminder to start the day."

Bee Lim jumped in noisily, "At least he didn't put the crap picture on our doors!"

"Excellent point. Well said," Simon replied, amused that the petite Asian woman had become such an eager participant, and then added, "Did you put one on your own door?"

"Of course, I am a member of this esteemed committee, am I not?" Andrew said with pride.

"Okay, we are all in this together," Simon stated, a little relieved that Andrew had included himself in the equation.

While this was going, on Buzzi had been drawing diligently on her pad with a red marker. She came prepared with color markers as well today. When she had finished her drawing, she tore the paper off and slid it onto the table.

CAUTION!

Excitedly, Andrew grabbed a pair of scissors and began to cut the drawing into the shape of a road sign, "I think I see where you are going. I like it."

Another picture soon appeared on the table and this was yesterday's picture of the crap with a 'Beware' written on it.

Simon looked over at Bee Lim, "Andrew may not have put up that drawing on our doors yesterday, but it looks like it is only a matter of time before he does."

Bee Lim stared at the picture and meekly smiled, "It seems to me we need to have a discussion ourselves here before we go outside this room with this."

They all looked up at her as her words struck home. She continued, "We should talk about our jobs and how serious we are with this before we go any farther. It may be costly!" She slowly lifted up the picture of the elephant with the 'Beware' on it. "Dealing with elephants starts in here, as far as I can tell. We started something yesterday and I think it had better continue!"

There was a sudden uneasy silence in the room. Just as Buzzi had cut through the crap yesterday, so Bee Lim cut through it today and put the issue on the table.

"It seems both of you are young and it is easy for you to find another job. Simon and myself are not in such a position ourselves. Can we talk about it?" Bee Lim continued.

Buzzi turned quickly to her pad and began to sketch out her thoughts. The group waited as she moved quickly over her paper. Finally she tore it off and put it on the table.

Buzzi then took her red pen and drew a red circle around it and then a line across it.

She looked at the group as if asking if that was what they wanted. The group looked at the picture and each other and slowly nodded their heads. 'Okay," Simon began, "A good reminder that we have agreed that there are to be no elephants in this room first and foremost? I guess that means we have to look at the different elephants we might be confronted by. Seems to me they may include finances, painful emotions, self-worth or loss of some kind. Where do we start?"

A dialogue began amongst us that put us all on edge for the rest of the meeting as we took turns to share about ourselves and what 'elephants' meant to us and our families. The key comments we heard were:

"I am too old to get trained to do another job. I won't be hired by another company and fear I will end up flipping burgers in some fast food joint."

"I must work as our family cannot survive on my husband's income. It isn't enough."

"Both my parents are dead and I have no one else. If I lose this job, I can't pay my bills."

"My wife has charged so much on our credit cards, if I lose this job, I may lose my house and probably her as well."

That day we all sat with the weight of a crucial decision upon us: should we deal with the real issues of a dying company? We all understood the cost to each of us as we listened to each other. We all knew that a cornered or dying animal was the most dangerous kind. Would the company be the same or actually want help? It seemed none of us knew the answer to that question.

Simon summed it up, "Okay, it seems like the pictures have pushed us to talk about difficult things in ways we might never otherwise have. So let's see what happens if we let these pictures loose on the company; let's see how others respond to them."

Bee Lim, Andrew and Buzzi nodded in agreement.

We drew together and organized some new signs that would be put out that night. As Andrew had admitted that he had put up the signs the previous night, it was his job to get them up before he left. Buzzi went to work to refine the signs that needed a real touch of art to catch people's attention.

It seems you must be very careful about experiencing real life and facing your fears. What had started the day before as honest laughter had an almost intoxicating effect on us. We had tasted something that was almost magic and for our own reasons, we were not willing to give it up.

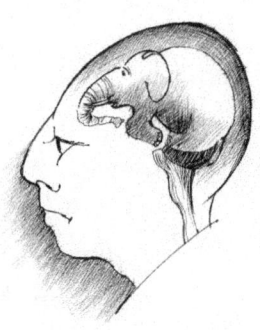

DAY THREE

Posters were planted all over the office that night. The day arrived as usual with people stumbling into their offices to trade hours for dollars. But on this day an excited buzz started to rise all over the offices. You could see people talking, with some stopping to stare at the signs, as if trying to figure out what it all meant. It was like a breath of fresh air had blown in and was stirring the stale and somewhat toxic air that hung heavily around them all.

Back in their inconspicuous corner of the building, the Change Committee sat around talking about people's reactions to their signs. Simon described a trip he took to the office of one of the directors to explain the posters, "I walked in and sat before the large cherry wood desk of Director Jones. He asked me to explain myself and our group and then, something came over me."

Simon hesitated here and looked at each of them, then continued, "I don't know what happened, but I saw each of you in my mind as we sat here and talked, and so I said to him, 'It seems like nobody talks around here. Like there are these huge elephants roaming freely all over this place and nobody wants to talk about them. Seems like you have to be so careful of all the elephant crap lying about, we thought it best to simply recognize what is going on. Marketing has no idea what Production is doing. Finance is always late giving us figures. In fact, we don't get any real information from anyone until it is too late or it is just simply safe but worthless data.'"

Bee Lim and Andrew looked over at Buzzi who had a huge smile on her face. They then stared at Simon who continued, "You know what the Director said?" They all shook their heads, "He said he wasn't sure pictures of elephants would really do anything, but it was about time someone around here started talking. Good job.'"

"While I sat there stunned, he nodded and I got up to leave. As I was walking out towards the door, he called out and said, 'You do know that if you mess this up, it's your job?'

I replied, 'Yes sir, and thank you for the honesty in mentioning that to me. I then turned and walked out. He had this smile on his face that I had never seen before."

Well, this was certainly cause for celebration. They all gave each other a high five. Andrew declared excitedly, "You're the man. You are the man."

Buzzi went to her pad and sketched out a drawing for Simon. She tore it from the pad and slid it onto the table.

An Elephant in the Room / 41

Simon looked at the picture and seemed to stand taller as he looked at it, "I haven't felt like this in years. I had almost forgotten what it was like to stand up at all."

They all eventually found their seats and sat back down.

"Wow, our first success, now what?" Bee Lim asked. She was feeling more confident.

"To be honest, I really have no idea as I have never done anything like this before… the floor is open to any ideas," Simon declared.

"Can we remind ourselves what the elephants stand for so we are all on the same page?" Andrew asked.

"It has to do with what we talk or maybe what we don't talk about," Bee Lim chimed in.

"Yeah, to me, it is about difficult conversations," Simon said.

Bee Lim reflected, "I wonder, why do we allow elephants? It seems like we don't want them, but then here they are."

Andrew was quick to answer, "It's the fault of our leaders. They are too preoccupied with themselves."

Simon responded, "That's too simple, Andrew. I have been with some of them in meetings and they really are trying to do their best. I can only look into myself and say it seems like I am uncomfortable with being vulnerable."

"In my family's culture, a big part of it is 'losing face'. You don't want to expose yourself to anyone so you try and hide things. I can see that but I didn't realize it might be in all cultures in a sense," Bee Lim added.

"Well, It seems like leaders play an important role in creating elephants. That's all I can see…" Andrew said a little defensively. He hesitated and then added, "and maybe… some fear in us, somewhere."

"Maybe that will be part of what we discover through this process… that the elephants reveal more about ourselves than we want to know? Let's see what happens," Simon said.

They all sat quietly for a few minutes and then somehow they all turned and looked at Buzzi. Sometime during the conversation she had started drawing.

At last Buzzi looked up and tore the page off her pad:

The other three gathered around and perused the drawing, which soon had them nodding in satisfaction. As they stood looking at the drawing, Buzzi went back to work.

Andrew stated, "It's like those road signs that say the road ahead is blocked and you can't get through. Only in this case you can't get through without talking about the elephants. I like it."

After a while, Buzzi finally tore off another picture from her pad and put it on the table.

Simon asked, "Mind if I say my thoughts as I look at your drawing?"

Buzzi wrote out, *'Go for it, any or all of you.'*

Simon continued, "Difficult conversations can clarify wonderful opportunities."

"I think it should say, 'To discover new opportunities, take only a 'safe' risk, if you must take a risk,'" Andrew smiled as he said this.

"A 'safe' risk? What does that mean… Oh, sorry, I get it now. There is no such thing as a safe risk," Bee Lim replied.

Andrew winked at Bee Lim before she had any time to feel stupid.

They all sat and looked at the pictures on the table for a few more minutes.

"Okay," Simon declared, "It looks like we have a couple of new images for tomorrow." He turned to Buzzi, "It seems like there is no way ahead without dialogue, and if we will work at dialogue, we may discover new opportunities."

"Do you think people will understand the implications of buying into these pictures?" wondered Bee Lim, with a worried look on her face, "We are asking people to change their entire way of doing things. Is that too much to ask?"

Simon quickly responded, "As Andrew joked earlier, it's a risk for us all. We are taking the risk and just asking them to join us."

Buzzi had a questioning look on her face and wrote out, *You sure you want to keep using my pictures?*

"Absolutely, I think we are all in agreement on that at least!" Simon stated, "We will just have to wait and see what happens next."

The committee then went to work discussing where the signs should go and who would put them where and when. They had got a nod of approval from Director Jones and were having too much fun to stop now.

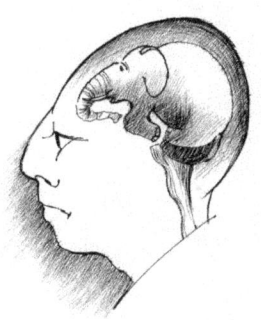

DAY FOUR

The signs were up and the buzz continued to grow among all the employees. They waited for the decree from the leaders to tell them what was going on. This usually meant a standard email with additions to the procedures manual to explain the change of 'policy'. Some people were checking their computers for emails every 10 minutes.

The Change Committee met at their appointed time and when all had taken their seats, Andrew jumped right in, "I had people coming by asking for the 'policy' email that is supposed to be sent out. You could see the look of fear in their eyes. Their little world was being shaken." Andrew was almost gleeful.

"That is our problem, isn't it?" Simon took a breath and thought out loud, "Okay, what does the manual or policy protect us from talking about?"

Andrew looked over at him and said with a smile, "Dude, you are a bit dangerous, my friend. You take this 'the crap stops here' seriously, don't you?"

"You can't upset people's worlds and pretend that nothing is going on. We challenged their world, we must help them to understand it and face it. That is part of the game plan. Hopefully they are getting the message that admitting that there is an elephant in the room is the first part of facing the changes that must be made," Simon stated as a matter of fact.

"How about a sign-up plan, a form of petition on the wall that people can sign if they want to get rid of the elephants?" Bee Lim asked. Her usual sense of caution seemed to require the participation of others in their cause.

"I like it," Andrew stated while Simon nodded his head and said, "It would give them an opportunity to agree with us in how we are trying to deal with the problems in our company."

Andrew added, "Can we put at the bottom of some of our pictures the statement, 'Change can only happen through dialogue.' This is for the staff who don't get the full meaning of our elephants and are wondering what we are doing."

"I was wondering about that as well. Let's do it," Simon said as he turned to Buzzi, "You're the one who is leading the creative charge here. We can't do it without you. Can you draw up something interesting?"

Buzzi nodded and sat for a second looking at her pad of paper. She looked up at the group and smiled, then went to work while the rest of the group chatted about their day in the office.

After a while, Buzzi slid the picture onto the table and looked at the others.

"Each of us is a boot?" Andrew asked and Buzzi nodded.

"So what does it mean to boot out an elephant?" Bee Lim asked.

Simon replied, "I think it means we face ourselves and where we are going."

'So we are honest about where we are or who we truly are and how we want to live. Then we talk about it.' Buzzi wrote out.

"It doesn't sound so profound for a change movement for the organization?" Bee Lim pondered out loud. She then looked around rather guiltily.

Simon took a deep breath and began to speak solemnly, "I have been here 25 years. We have created an organizational culture that, like slowly heating water that eventually boils the frog alive, seduces us so that we see the slow loss of our voice, the loss of communication or relationship, as something not to worry about. It seems to whisper to us all, 'Don't deal with it now. It is a small thing and not that important.' Slowly the elephants were born and they are now effecting a slow but sure death. I am starting, I must admit, only starting, to see this for the first time in my life."

Andrew mumbled barely audibly, "25 years, dude, that is a long time. A slow death for 25 years. I'm sure you're…"

Simon interrupted, "You are in it too, right now. I think that is what we are fighting against, with the boots."

A silence fell over the Change Committee as they thought of the work ahead.

Simon asked, "We sign the boots, I am assuming?" and Buzzi nodded and then, she leaned over and signed her name on one of the boots. Simon asked, "May I?" Buzzi handed him her pencil and he signed it as well. He passed the pencil to Andrew who signed it and then Bee Lim, who sighed before signing her name in her neat handwriting.

'So now we need the people in the company to sign it as well!' Buzzi wrote out. It was an exciting thought to have others share in their desire for change.

We each got to work and laid out our plans for the next day. The life in the room was like a fire that gave warmth to us all. There was also a sense that a fire could be scary as well, if its power was not respected.

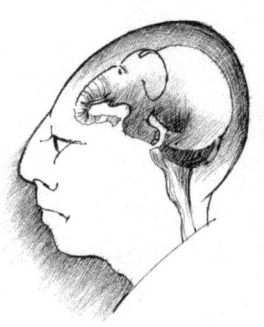

DAY FIVE

Andrew had gone out that night and found an all-night printer and done his work. The following morning, the staff drifted to work and saw the posters up on the wall. Anyone entering the building simply could not miss the posters. There were also posters put up all over the building.

As Andrew, Bee Lim, Buzzi and Simon each entered the building at different times, they made sure to stop and look at the poster next to the receptionist. It was a larger version of the picture of the elephant's backside with large boots all around it as if kicking it out.

A small group of people was standing in front of the poster talking quietly about it when Bee Lim walked in. She hesitated for a brief moment and then walked over to the receptionist, "May I borrow the largest marker you have?"

The receptionist handed her a large black marker and Bee Lim stood tall (as tall as she could, that is) in her high heels and walked over and signed one of the boots. She then turned and looked at the group standing there, "I have already signed it but I don't think I signed it big enough. It seems to me that we must start a dialogue among ourselves and talk about the things we have been avoiding for years. Anyone else care to sign up to boot the elephants from our company?"

The crowd of people looked awkwardly at each other. Finally, an older woman at the back of the group pushed her way forward. She took the marker and signed a boot and said, "I have been here as long as anyone and I am tired of all the supposed 'secrets' that everyone knows. Glad to join you in the fight." The older woman had a stern look on her face and turned to face the small group. She challenged them, "Any one else got the guts to join us?" Slowly, a young girl carrying a clipboard followed and then, everyone else took the marker and signed it.

"Well done, thank you," Bee Lim said warmly as each person signed it. She was trying not to breathe hard from the effort of behaving rather unlike her usual self. Finally, the last person gave the marker back to the receptionist.

"Have a good day," Bee Lim chirped and then walked down the hall towards Finance. She didn't dare turn around but if anyone could have seen her face, they would have seen her beaming from ear to ear.

•••

The Change Committee met in their usual corner at the back of the building. Few people knew where they met; though the buzz was growing in the company, none would have guessed it was emanating from there *(most people thought we were power brokers with key roles in the company but we knew better)*.

As they all walked, in Buzzi was already busy at work on her pad and they sat down to wait for her picture.

Bee Lim asked, "Simon, did you get a call from the Directors at all?"

"No. To be honest, I was expecting a call or an email, but they have said nothing to me. So we'll have to see what happens in the next couple of days as there is definitely a growing awareness of us."

Bee Lim described her arrival at work and she got a standing ovation from Simon and Andrew.

Buzzi slid a sketch onto the table in front of Simon.

Buzzi then slid a picture in front of Andrew.

And she then slid a picture in front of Bee Lim.

Each sat silently looking at the picture in front of them.

"You know where to poke that little pencil of yours, don't you? You seem to home in on the soft spot and go for it," Simon said ruefully.

"But this is work, we don't talk about personal things at work, do we? I thought the first day was just a once-off thing?" Bee Lim asked. Her earlier confidence was being threatened by the prospect of personal vulnerability.

Andrew looked around the room at each of them and then at last said, "I don't have any place else to talk. No one else is listening to me right now, except in here. I wouldn't mind talking, if you would listen?"

Andrew's unexpected offer broke the tension. Simon reached over and took Buzzi's hand and said, "I am not objecting to your little pencil being such a strong voice. You fit in here and we couldn't do what we do without you. Thank you for asking and challenging us again."

They all watched as tears formed and then slowly slid down Buzzi's face. She looked at each of them and the tears just dropped freely onto her pad of paper.

If we had known Buzzi a little bit better, we would have known she had never belonged to any group or felt included before.

As a precious silence settled over the team, Buzzi looked down at the pictures she had sketched earlier and then looked up seriously at them.

Again, Andrew was the first to respond, "I don't know what to say; whatever I say, she just says I don't mean it."

Simon sighed, "How can I tell my daughter, who is now a young woman, what a fool I have been, when she hasn't listened to me in years?"

Bee Lim said simply, "You don't talk about some things in my family or culture. If you talk about these undiscussable things, that is a huge loss of face and so you just don't do it."

And so they moved from laughter on the first day to tears. Each wept as they shared their struggles with their relationships. For the first time in many years they knew that their hearts had been heard. It was as if someone else knowing their struggle and pains made them more bearable.

Buzzi pulled out her pad and put it on the table. She pointed at the little wrinkled marks that her tears had made and pointed at each of them and then pointed at the elephants.

All knew that Buzzi was speaking directly to them. They had their work cut out for them. Very difficult conversations were ahead and they knew it. Simon summed it up by saying, "I guess it's about time. We need to deal with elephants at home if we want to deal effectively with those here. I guess our work here will have to wait until tomorrow. Let's, for once, with joy and it looks like, in tears, take our work home with us!"

Bee Lim and Andrew nodded while Buzzi's glowing smile confirmed what she thought.

We had never imagined that you could find a place at work with people who really cared and would be willing to listen. Miracles in life can happen at work. Our hope was that a miracle could also happen at home, even in the deepest reaches of the human heart.

We were to find that the most powerful change is rooted in honesty, for once seeing things as they are and not as we want or expect them to be.

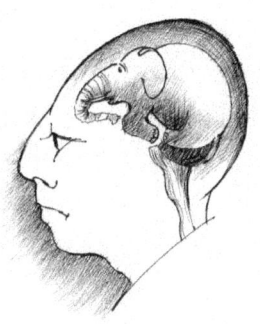

DAY SIX

As Simon walked into the building the next day, he didn't get to his office before different people stopped him and asked him what was going on, "Did you guys get stopped?" "There are no more pictures, what happened?"…

Simon assured them that there were more to come before settling in his office to catch up with paperwork. But a call from the Director asking to see him left him wondering if the questions he had just heard from others were predicting the outcome of the meeting.

Simon walked into Director Jones' office and sat down. The Director sat, looked at him and stated bluntly, "I still find it hard to imagine that some pictures of elephants are creating all these waves! Tell me again what you are thinking and why you think this is working?"

Simon looked out the window and reflected for a moment, and then said, "First, to be honest, I am not sure why this is happening. I have been thinking and reading about change, trying to figure it out. In actual fact, it seems more like we stumbled upon it. All I can say is that there is a power in dialogue that seems to have a life in it that I never thought possible. Our words seem to have a power to move us and when we can't or don't talk about things we care about, we get all stopped up and start to die... I am not sure if that makes a lot of sense?"

The Director said, "Hmm, I don't know and I am not sure I even care about the theory except that, to my utter amazement, it is working. People are more engaged and departments are talking with each other. Or, maybe I should say it 'was' working. I didn't see anything new today, is your team backing off?"

Simon shook his head, "No sir, we just took a break to have some long-needed conversations at home. We will have more material for tomorrow."

"Okay, can I give you some advice?"

"I would hope so, sir."

It was the Director's turn to look out the window for a second. "I have been wondering about, maybe even dreading, this. I knew it had to happen. The Board just called me in and said that the little Change Committee had to cool it or else."

"What did you say, sir?" Simon asked as he wiped the perspiration from his face.

"I told them I would look into it," the Director smiled for a moment and said, "There are some fearsome elephants in that room and just between you and me, it wasn't the time to take them on just yet."

"I understand, sir."

"Call me Jimmy, Simon. It seems we are now in this together. I have been telling them that we are dying for years but the family that owns most of our stock wants to wring out every ounce of blood before they bury us. They know our market share is a free lunch for anyone who wants it but they just don't seem to care. I am not ready to die, how about you?"

Simon smiled, "It is the first time I have felt alive in years. I am not willing to roll over and die just yet. What would you like us to do, sir?

"Call me Jimmy, please. I would like you to hit the staff your message hard and fast. I think I can give us two or maybe three days before I get called in again. I need everyone alive and ready for action by then, if you know what I mean?"

"I do, sir, and my team and I will put everything we have into this. Just don't get caught in the stampede of elephants, if you know what I mean."

"Good advice, Simon. Now get down there with your fantastic little team and see if you can keep this 'awakening' going and people talking even more."

Simon got up and looked at the Director and said, "Thank you, sir, I mean… er… Jimmy." He then turned and walked out the door and immediately called the team and told them they needed to meet at the 'office' in half an hour's time.

•••

The team gathered in their corner office and sat down. Buzzi, Andrew and Bee Lim were all quiet and waited for Simon to catch them up on what had happened. Simon gave them the details of his meeting with Director Jones.

They all sat quietly for a few moments, thinking about the questions the Director had asked about moving forward. Bee Lim finally stated, "It is what you mentioned yesterday, Simon. It seems like we all want to be heard and to have a voice. You take that from us and something precious in us dies."

A few more moments of silence and then Simon sighed, "Well said, Bee Lim." He took a slow breath and played with his glasses and then continued, "I hope we will have time later to figure this out, but for now, we have work to do. That is why I called the meeting early. We must get to work right away. I'm afraid we don't even have time to talk about how our 'homework' went. Would anyone mind if we jumped right into this and caught up later?"

They all agreed the 'homework' could wait except Buzzi. She shook her head and pointed at her pad.

"Okay, Buzzi, what do you want to do, because we are not going forward without you?" Simon asked.

Buzzi wrote on a piece of paper, *'I have a gift I drew for you. It is about our time yesterday.'* She pulled out three pieces of paper. *'I made a copy for each of you.'* She slid a piece of paper on the table in front of each of them.

Simon, Andrew and Bee Lim looked long at their 'gift'. Finally Bee Lim spoke, "Out of our tears grows life." Andrew mumbled, "Hmmm, Beauty out of pain?" Simon continued, "In the midst of suffering, we grow up."

Buzzi beamed at each of them.

Bee Lim declared, "What can you say after that?"

Andrew mumbled, "I agree with it in principle, but I think pain is highly over-rated." He gave a rueful smile.

Simon shot Andrew a look and then said, "Okay, Buzzi, I trust you don't mind hitting the pad, so to speak, as we need a few different drawings and then we need to get them out. Can you do it?"

Buzzi slowly nodded her head and wrote in reply, *'I was born ready for this day. Just turn me loose as I have been thinking a lot about this.'*

"Consider yourself 'loosed', Buzzi. Also, If you don't mind, the rest of us will put our heads together to see if we can come up with some words to enhance the effect of your drawings." Simon said.

'You do it your way and I will do it mine. Consider yourself 'loosed'!' Buzzi wrote back.

"Thank you," Simon replied as he sat to work with Andrew and Bee Lim to put words together while Buzzi put her pencil to work.

The next few hours slipped past us in a hurry. Slowly, we formed our ideas into words and images. Finally we were ready to present our ideas.

Bee Lim stood before everyone, cleared her throat and said, "We tried to put together a group of sayings but they all seemed to be so clichéd compared to the images, so we thought we would try and use just one saying. Let me show you what we have finally settled on". Bee Lim held up a card:

If you can't talk about it,
You can't change it.

Bee Lim looked over at Andrew and continued, "On a side note, Andrew found this quote by Thomas Merton that he really liked. It goes:

> The truth that many people never understand, until it is too late, is that the more you try to avoid suffering the more you suffer because smaller and more insignificant things begin to torture you in proportion to your fear of being hurt."[1]

Andrew jumped in, "What I got from this is that if you fear confrontation or difficult conversations, then that fear will get bigger and bigger, and produce the elephants that will cause greater damage than the original fear would have."

Simon looked over at Andrew, "Well said Andrew."

"Thanks," Andrew replied.

'I like it. Great job.' Buzzi wrote.

Bee Lim asked, "Now how about your ideas?"

Buzzi stood up before the others. She tore off some pages and then put them one by one on the table. As she did this, she wrote out, *'I think these posters deal with how poorly we communicate.'*

Buzzi slid the first picture over for everyone to see.

Simon asked, "Can we talk about what the pictures mean to us as we see them? We did this once before and it was really effective."

'Bring it on. That would help me,' Buzzi wrote back.

"Mediocrity rules when you won't face the elephants," Andrew called out.

"We have abandoned quality because of our unwillingness to talk," Bee Lim offered.

"How about, the quality of a product can only be measured by the clarity of the dialogue of those who created it?" Simon asked.

Buzzi gave them all a thumbs-up.

She pulled out another sketch and showed it to them.

"Go for the quick or easy fix," Simon responded.

"Truth is good as long as it makes no one feel uncomfortable," Bee Lim reflected as she gigled at how funny the elephant looked trying to hide behind the sign, and then thought of how funny she must have looked many times, trying to hide herself in embarrassing situations.

"The devil made me do it. Blame it on him!" Andrew declared as the others turned and looked at him in amusement. "So much for 'getting the best' from people, Mr. Human Resource!" Simon said ironically.

Buzzi quickly pulled out another picture.

Bee Lim quietly stated, "Keep real evaluations hidden."

"Say only what you think people want you to say. Don't let the facts confuse you," Simon declared.

"People's self-esteem is too fragile. The truth will crush them. The most important thing is for people to feel happy about themselves…" Andrew said with a hint of cynicism.

They all sat silently for a moment, thinking about the work ahead. Simon said finally, "Great work. You are brilliant. May I ask that you add a boot on each of the posters that will stand for our signature?"

Buzzi nodded as she grabbed the sketches and added a boot on them as the group's signature.

"Great idea, Simon," Andrew declared.

We got down to work that day. We each took to our respective tasks of organizing, printing, scouting locations and planning for the next day. There was a flurry of activity as we all recognized how important it was to get the material out as soon as possible.

Later, when they were ready for the next day, Simon closed the meeting, "Okay, well done, everyone. I think we will need some more ideas for elephant posters for tomorrow, so if anyone has any ideas, please text Buzzi. Otherwise, our creative artist, can you put together four or five more for tomorrow and we will get them out in our last push?"

Buzzi nodded in agreement and the group broke up to get the work done.

As they were leaving, Simon said, "I have one more idea. How about lunch tomorrow to continue our personal dialogue?"

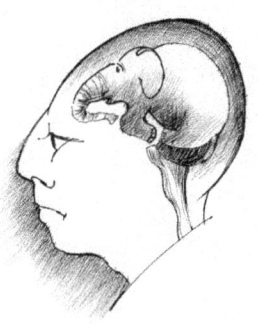

DAY SEVEN

The Change Committee met at its usual time and was going over the day with each other. The day had been busy addressing questions and pushing people towards dialogue.

Some of the comments that were shared in conversations all over the company were:

"I hear Marketing and Sales are meeting together for the first time in a year to actually talk."

"Old Ed, from Quality was talking to Customer Service and they were actually listening to each other. They actually listened to some of the phones calls from customers and couldn't believe what they were hearing about the products… The two departments are now working on a plan to connect more often."

"I hear Training is now developing programs around communication and dialogue. It will be the focus for the whole year."

"I actually got my team from Production in the same room as Purchasing and we just got the chance to get to know each other. By the end of the meeting, they had actually raised several concerns and frustrations of their department. It was the first really honest conversation since… since I don't know when."

"I even got some comments from the cleaners who had seen the art work and decided to add their thoughts into the mix."

Periodically the team would stop and shout out or whoop or do a little dance (that was Buzzi). Stories and comments just seemed to pour out and they couldn't stop for a while as it was just too much fun.

Simon finally raised his hand and said, "Okay, I know there is more but we have to get some work done as we may only have one day left before the proverbial crap hits the fan. Buzzi, how are you doing with your sketches?"

Buzzi smiled and opened her pad. She wrote on it, *'Thank you for the ideas you sent me, they were very helpful. Just to let you know, I received something from everyone.'*

Andrew, Bee Lim and Simon all looked at each other and smiled, and Bee Lim said, "It was actually fun. What did you do with them? We are dying to see the end product."

'First I have another small gift for each of you.' Buzzi reached into her bag and pulled out a small pair of boots with Simon's name on it and gave it to him. She also gave one to Andrew with his name on it. Then she reached into her bag and pulled out a tiny pair of high heels with Bee Lim's name on it and gave it to her. Last, she pulled out a pair of slippers with her own name on it and pinned it on the front of her shirt. She wrote out, *'The Change Committee now has formal name tags to identify itself.'*

As the others put on their creative name tags with great enthusiasm, Buzzi wrote, *'Okay, I took some of your comments and my own thoughts, and tried to draw some sketches to get the ideas across. So here they are. It seems to me that there are three different categories and this first category will focus on how we think as an organization.'*

Buzzi pointed to Simon to indicate where the idea came from as she slid the first drawing onto the table.

Simon chuckled, "I think the words I said were, 'Opportunities are ignored and we call them threats.' But I agree with Andrew that a picture is worth a thousand words. Let me make sure I get it. So you may have a large feast if you want to face the elephants or a simple meal without facing the elephants?"

Buzzi nodded.

Andrew declared, "Grab what you can now because no one knows what will happen tomorrow."

Simon jumped in again, "After I see the picture and think about it, I would say, 'focus on the short term results at the expense of better and more permanent outcomes'?"

Bee Lim reflected out loud, "I like this one. We have been focused on quick results, the quick financial statement that makes us look good, but we are eating away at our assets as there is no investment in the long term." Bee Lim hesitated, "Hmm, but to deal with this would require leaders to look beyond their short leadership cycle. Well, that would certainly require some very difficult conversations that would affect egos and reputations... Yikes!"

Then Buzzi held up two pictures at the same time. She looked back and forth at them to show she didn't know which one she liked better.

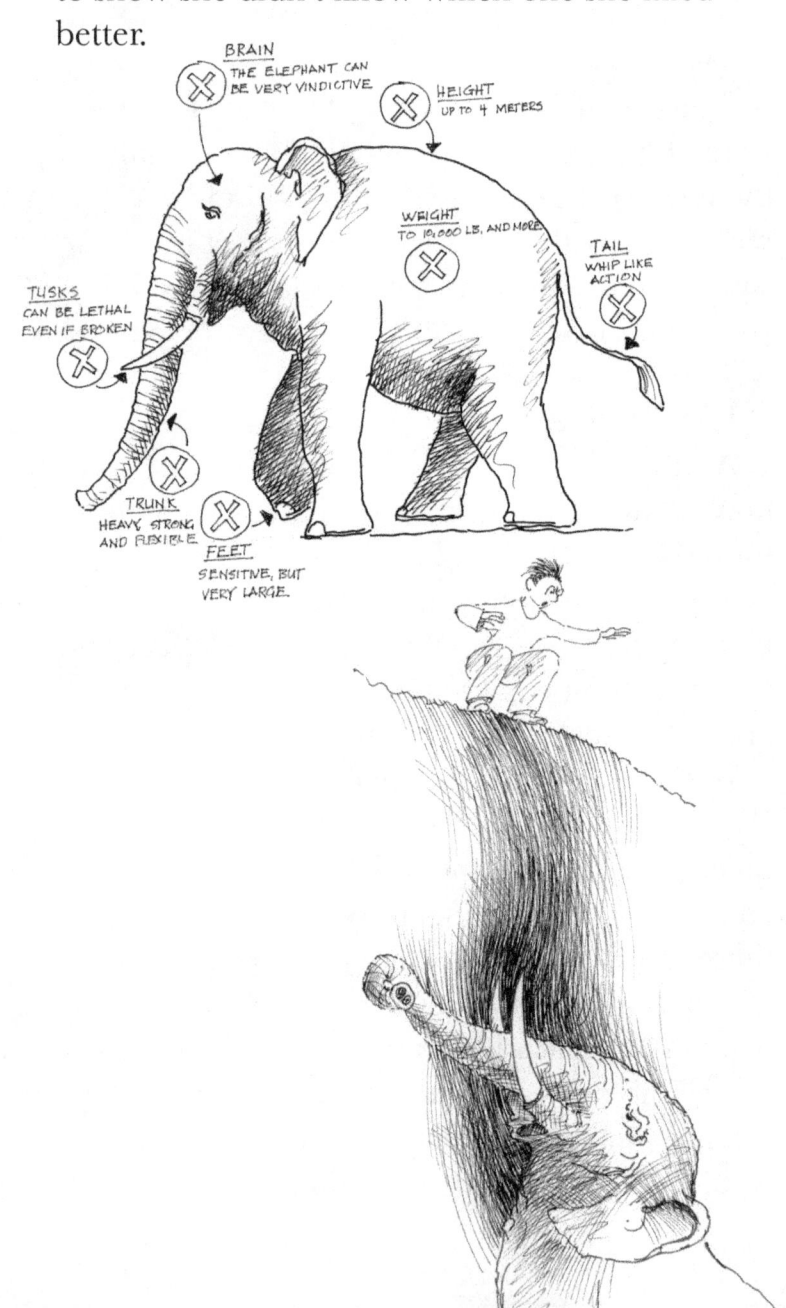

These pictures prompted a barrage of thoughts that sounded rapidly through the air:

"Don't look down, whatever you do… *don't* look down," Andrew said in mock fear.

"You find what you are looking for!" Bee Lim stated.

Andrew continued on, "Tell me again how many ways he could hurt me! Focus more on the pain please!"

"Some people tread cautiously through life so that they may arrive safely at death's door," Simon called out with a smile on his face.

A silence hung in the room and then Simon said, rather eloquently, "When we focus on the fear of elephants, we lose perspective of what we are losing by their presence. We are losing success, opportunity, beauty, honor, creativity, and money. How sad is that?"

Buzzi pulled out another group of pictures and wrote out, *'This group of pictures deals with how we organize.'*

Andrew exclaimed, "Wow, I like that! That sums up my day. Everyone brings me all their problems and thinks that it is HR's job to deal with them because they don't want to have to talk to the real people they have the issues with. I want as many copies of this picture as I can get. Can I get that put on my door with a saying, 'clean up your own crap… please?'"

"Hmmm, Andrew, it may not be the most effective way to encourage people. How about you wait until they get in your office and then have a conversation with them about it?" Simon asked, barely hiding a smile.

"Ouch, I can see that would be hard work." Andrew said, looking a little uncertain all of a sudden, "Now I remember why there are so many elephants as this could be a real challenge. Are we sure we want to go down this path? I mean, we will have to do it ourselves, right?"

Buzzi pulled out another picture.

"Has anyone read the company manual…?" Andrew answered his own question, "Not ever! No never!"

"To me, this is not about the company manual, it's about teaching people who come into the company to recognize the elephants and keep away from upsetting them. It's about helping people to know what we cannot talk about," Bee Lim stated as she looked over at Andrew

"I agree with Bee Lim," Simon stated, "Oh, I remember when I first joined the company and I was naive enough to mention my desire to have my own corner office one day. You would have thought someone died. There are just some things you don't say."

Buzzi slid her next picture onto the table to keep the conversation moving forward.

"Smurfs, a kingdom of Smurfs. That's all this is," Andrew was the first to respond.

"The trails the elephants create form natural boundaries to how we relate to each other and indicate who is in control of certain areas," Simon stated.

Bee Lim jumped in, "The elephants remind us of our fears and we get defensive and protective and use our little power base to protect ourselves."

"Okay, how about a game of Risk, anyone? This makes me want to take over the world," Andrew said as he stood up like a leader ready to take his troops to war.

Buzzi grinned at the comments and put out another idea.

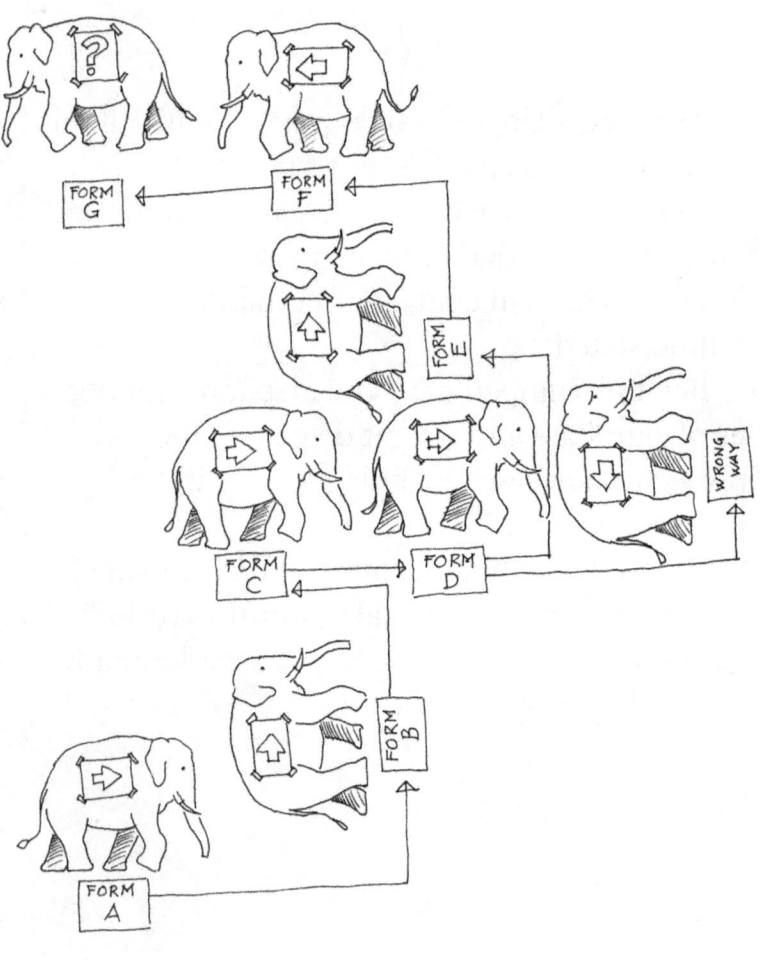

By now, the Change Committee was really getting excited and could hardly wait to give their comments.

"Have I filled out form 29A for the application for the permit to eat at this table for lunch?" Andrew asked, grabbing a pen like he wanted to sign a piece of paper.

Before anyone else could say anything, Andrew continued, "How do you say 'cover my a--'? Why, you say it with paper work, of course."

"All I can hear are my boss' words, 'Make sure you have a paper trail.' I hear that all the time and now I can see it in a whole new light," Simon added.

Buzzi pulled out yet another picture and put it on the table.

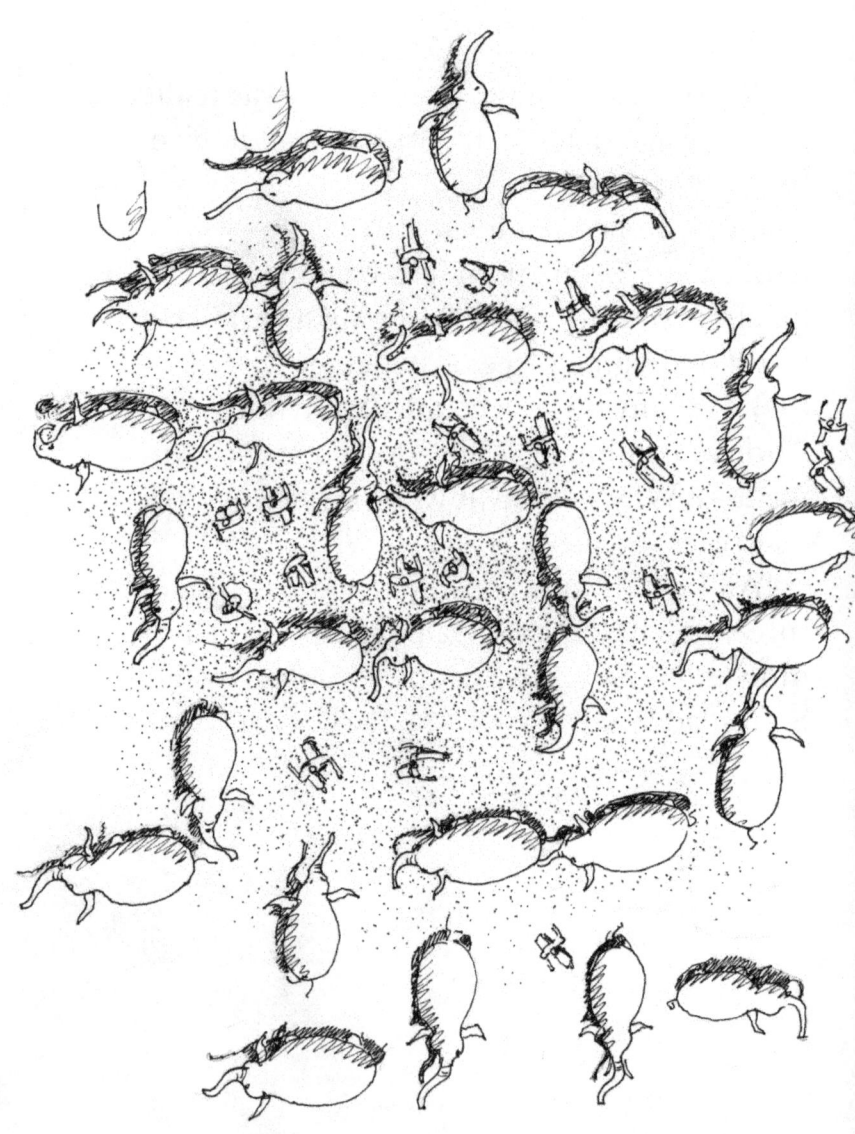

Simon pondered out loud, "The thing I love about this picture is that there is so much here, it takes me a while to get it all." He continued seriously, " I think about all the elephants at large, and how we are so busy trying to avoid them because of what we think might happen, we have no idea what not dealing with them is really doing to us right now."

Bee Lim said, "That is our finance department. No one wants to question or inquire into how money is being spent so we don't say anything and end up spending half our day doing things in a round about way when a simple conversation could clear it all up."

Andrew piped in, "Look at how well the elephants have trained us. We do exactly what they want." He hesitated and then said, "They show us were we can and cannot go."

Buzzi gave another thumbs up and wrote out, *'This last group deals with conflict and how we deal with it.'* She then pulled out another group of sketches. She turned the first one over.

"Create a crisis to get anything done," Andrew declared.

Simon said, "If you want something done, scare the people and while everyone is terrified, do what you want quickly while no one is looking. That way you don't have to have any difficult conversations about it."

"The only way to get money around here is to say you have a crisis. I can't tell you how many times I hear about a crisis in different departments. It's like a free ticket to money they need without having to talk about where the crisis came from and what really needs to be done," Bee Lim stated.

Buzzi pulled out a new sketch.

'This idea was from Andrew', Buzzi wrote as she blew Andrew a kiss.

"Hey, I just said job descriptions are more of a pain if people want to hide and don't want to talk about them. I didn't say it nearly that well," Andrew replied, pointing at the picture.

"That's good. We use a good thing, our job description, to protect us from being vulnerable. The only problem is that I can see myself doing that at times. This is painful, you know?" Simon mumbled humbly. Andrew nodded vigorously in agreement.

"We are not saying job descriptions are wrong, are we? I had to fight just to get one," Bee Lim said in sudden alarm.

"No, just that they need to be a living thing, like a container, if you will, to hold the ongoing conversations about what we do," Andrew stated strongly.

Everyone turned and looked at him. Bee Lim said admiringly, "Why Andrew, that is a really good way to say it."

Andrew smiled, "Hey, I have thought long and hard about this. You have no idea how many mundane hours I have spent on job descriptions that are a waste of time because of all the issues people won't talk about."

Buzzi pulled out another sketch and pointed at Bee Lim from whom the idea had apparently come.

"I have some cynics in my office who seem stuck where they are. I can almost hear them saying, 'It's no use, the elephants will come back anyway'," Bee Lim replied.

Simon said with a painful expression, "I can see the look in their eyes. They are almost indifferent or maybe too self-satisfied to commit to conflict."

"Hey, how about we leave blanks on some of these pictures, maybe with quotation marks, and ask people to fill in what the image says to them? That will get them involved," Andrew interjected suddenly.

"Great idea," Simon said, "Let's do it."

Andrew said, "I would write, 'Make peace, not war.'"

Buzzi pulled out another picture and wrote out, *'Last one.'*

"The buck stops… there!" Andrew snorted and then continued, "You want me to make a tough decision? Do I look that stupid?"

"Unless you own the company, don't even think about making that decision," Simon said, with a hint of disgust as he had seen this particular manoeuvre happen many times.

"Tough decisions are never made, until they are passed up as high as possible," Bee Lim with frustration.

Buzzi held out her hands as if to say, that's it.

Bee Lim, Andrew and Simon all agreed that Buzzi had outdone herself.

After a while, we all settled into our seats and mapped out our plan for the next 24 hours. The strategy came together slowly as we listened to each other.

"Let me summarize," Simon stated, "We will keep churning out our posters all day and distributing them to different parts of the company. Buzzi, as soon as you get one done, you pass it on to Andrew who will make copies and get them out. Bee Lim will monitor them to see who is reading them and I will be the buffer for when we hear from the Directors." His tone changed, "Oh, and before we finish, may I invite all of you to my house this Saturday night? The whole family is invited. My daughter has even agreed to come."

"Wow, that would be great. I will even bring my wife, who is now interested in going out with me," Andrew smiled as he said this.

"My husband doesn't speak the best English, you know, but he'll be there!" Bee Lim declared.

Buzzi stood up and wrote out, *'I don't 'speak' any English myself so he'd better come, and bring your two little girls, Wee San and CeCe. I must see them.'* Bee Lim nodded and smiled at Buzzi, "He would love to come and meet you. I have told him all about you and he has been begging to meet you all."

"Okay, it is a deal, my house this Saturday at 6pm. We'll have a barbeque. Now, let's keep this thing going as long as we can," Simon declared with a determined look in his eye.

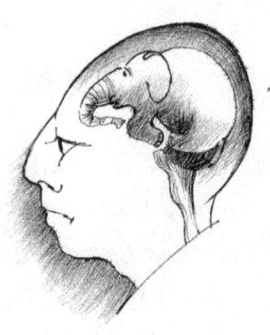

DAY EIGHT

Simon drove over to pick up Buzzi to give her a lift to work. He wanted to make sure she was dealing with the pressure of her drawings being put on display. They both agreed they were having the time of their lives. As they walked in together, there was a small group standing looking at the latest drawings and then they turned and looked at Buzzi and Simon.

One of them called out, "Hey Simon, who did the art work? It's great."

Simon turned and pointed to Buzzi who was almost standing behind him. He pulled her out and said, "She is brilliant at turning ideas into pictures."

The small group of people standing by the picture then did the most amazing thing, they clapped for her, not just a polite clap, but a loud one, and then a voice yelled out, "Thank you."

Buzzi nodded and then quickly scurried off towards her office. Simon walked past the group and said, "Thank you. She was speechless," and then walked on with a smile on his face.

When he got to his office, there was a note on his desk to go straight to Director Jones' office. He set his briefcase down, turned right around, and went upstairs.

The secretary let him in and the Director pointed to the usual chair, "Come on in, Simon, and thank you for coming right up. It seems we are in a bit of a jam and I can't hold it back anymore."

"May I ask what that is?" Simon asked. His mind was already racing, thinking of all sorts of scenarios.

"Of course. I have a meeting tonight with the family and other Directors. It seems they have had enough. I'm not sure if I can keep all our jobs but if we buckle quickly, I think we can stay for a while."

"Sir, may I speak honestly?"

"I would expect nothing else of you, Simon, please."

"Okay, Jimmy. I can't back down. I won't speak for the team but I am fairly sure we have come this far and would not be willing to stop what we have started. I'm afraid we are going to push as long as we can. I can't tell you how much fun it has been."

"You know, Simon, I was thinking you might say that. Actually, I was hoping you might say that. So I called Channel 2 news and they are going to do a feature on you tonight. I told them about the group and especially about Buzzi, and they were very interested in the story."

"How did you find out about her? We sensed we were selected as a bunch of unknowns who would be easy scapegoats."

"You underestimate yourselves. I did my own homework last night trying to find a way forward. I thought the city might like some local heroes who are going to save an old institution in this town. What do you think? You game?"

"I must ask the group's permission but I assume they would love the extra push from the media and it might also give you a bit of leverage with the elephants in your meeting tonight."

The Director nodded his head, "Exactly. I need all the help I can get but I think we have enough momentum to keep this thing going."

"Thank you for your support, Jimmy."

"It is I that should be thanking you. I have been waiting for this opportunity for years and you have given it to me, finally. I never saw it coming. I will thank you all at the press conference in one hour's time. Be at the main lobby then, okay?"

Simon stood up and began to leave, "Thank you. Yes, I had better get going as there is a lot to do in the next short hour. I will see you then."

Simon quickly made the calls and asked the team to come to his office in fifteen minutes. They all made it and Simon quickly gave them most of the information he had. He then said, "Oh yeah, and we have a press conference with Channel 2 news in 25 minutes."

All their eyes grew large and Andrew said, "No, you're kidding?"

Bee Lim looked at her clothes and shoes and murmured, "I wish I had known; I would have worn something different."

Buzzi wrote out quickly, *'Yeah me too. These jeans are not my favorite ones… wait, they're all I have…'*

They all laughed.

Then Simon gave out instructions, "Andrew, go and get five or six of the drawings from around the building. Bee Lim, make sure that the big sign at the entrance is up and looks good. All of us need our badges on as well. Buzzi, can you gather or re-sketch some of the work you have done and review what we have walked through in the last week? We will use those to tell our story. Okay? Let's move it, folks."

With that, we all headed off to get ready before the cameras arrived.

We basically told them what we have told you here. I think they really liked the first picture with the words 'the crap stops here'. They had a close up of that on TV. I might add that Bee Lim looked beautiful, Andrew looked smart, Simon looked distinguished and, well, I just looked like me.

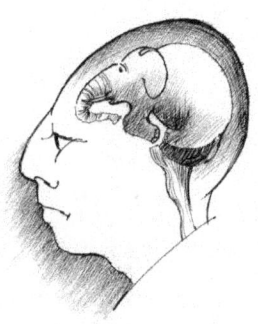

EPILOGUE

I guess you might want to know what happened to us after the conference. I warned you that this was a condensed version of our story. I never have been much for words, but you might have guessed that already.

The news conference was a smash and our company was the talk of the town. The owners couldn't really bleed it then so they gave Director Jones freedom to try some new things and our company began to turn around.

We were done before we even started. None of us were change experts, just people with a desire to be honest and real, with gifts that we were willing to risk using in our own unique way. We quickly realized that we needed trainers to come in and teach us all how to communicate as we had forgotten how. It worked.

We had a great meal at Simon's house. It took us all of two minutes to get over the initial awkwardness of it all. It was like we had known each other for years. We talked or wrote until well past midnight (although Simon looked dead tired by then… I don't think he is much of a night owl.)

Our Change Committee was disbanded and we missed each other a lot. Then I got a call from another company and they asked for help. I referred them to my "partner" (Simon didn't know it yet, but he was getting used to change by then) and he pulled in Bee Lim and Andrew for Finance and Marketing (Andrew always said he wanted to market something).

I guess we were better at change than we thought. Some people even call us experts, imagine that.

Stop by and see us if you want. We love the friendships.

I didn't show you the picture I drew for the team as a 'gift'. I wanted to save it for here:

Remember, in your suffering and pain, the only way out is to begin a dialogue. If you want to change anything, you must start by talking about it.

I trust you will discover, in your tears, that through openness and honesty, the struggle will give birth to beauty and life. Out of the ashes of life, God wants to bring beauty.

God bless you.

Picture This Communications

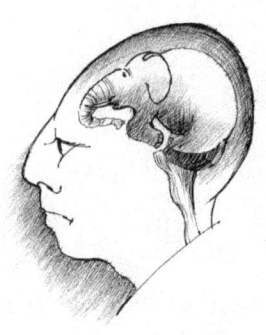

APPENDIX A
How to face an elephant?

Acknowledge that there are elephants.

Discover what it costs you to allow the elephants to be there. You must want something more than you fear the elephant or you will be stuck in the situation until you hit a crisis, when it is often too late to deal with the elephants.

Identify what specifically is undiscussable? Accept that your 'version' of the undiscussable issue may be part of the problem.

Admit what <u>your reaction</u> is to the issue. (Think hard about the following questions:) What are the facts? (Be specific in your thinking. This is the data that everyone involved would agree is a part of the issue.)

What is your interpretation of the facts?
What do they mean to you?
What assumptions have you made to fill in the missing pieces?
What are your emotions?
Where are you being defensive?
What is threatening or embarrassing about the issue?
Own these things going on in you as a part of your own life.

Assess what you want from this situation.
Explore what others might want from this situation.
Clarify where you (or your organization) are going and what you need to talk about to get there.

Engage those involved in the issue. Bring as much of your (see above) reaction to the issue into the dialogue as is possible. This is hard work and requires discipline and risk, but it is worth the investment.

If you are stuck, go back to the start above.

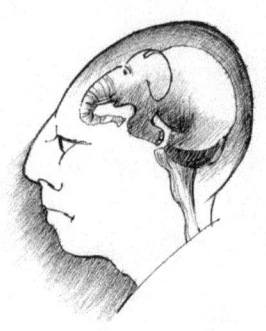

AUTHOR'S NOTE

What I have tried to give in this simple story is a guideline for how to look at change. There are all kinds of techniques and programs out there that deal with change. It can be overwhelming and confusing. However, you can be sure that any program you are using that involves open and honest dialogue is moving you in the right direction. Any program that focuses just on techniques and technical issues but does not involve dialogue is moving you in the wrong direction. There are no 'perfect' programs but there are clear directions any leader must take. I trust you can see as a result of this story that the foundation for any change program must be built on dialogue.

One of the simplest and yet most important keys to changing a company, team or even yourself, is clear and honest communication. I wanted people to think about the painful effects of not communicating. Few people realize how quickly not talking about something can destroy a relationship, team or organization. Simply put, how we talk to and with each other is one of the single most powerful elements that define how good, honest, real and successful our relationships are. As relationships go, so go our teams and organizations. And in the end, so goes life.

Most people think that if you can talk, you can communicate. That would be like thinking that because you can move, you could run a marathon. It could be a disastrous mistake. There is some training that must take place. One of the most important skills we all must develop is in the area of clear and honest dialogue, especially engaging in difficult conversations. If you don't feel confident, seek wisdom, as there are some excellent trainers out there.

We can change our world but it will only happen - one effective conversation at a time.

I can be contacted at: mrawlins@mac.com

I will be setting up a site for this book at: anelephantintheroom.com.

I have written some books that might help you learn more about communication and change. Some of them include:

The Green Bench – A dialogue about leadership and change

The Green Bench II – Ongoing dialogue about leadership and communication

The Lottery – How a question can change a life.

A few other good books I would suggest are:

Dialogue by William Isaacs

Crucial Conversations by Kerry Patterson, Joseph Grenny, Ron McMillan, Al Switzler

Difficult Conversations by Douglas Stone, Bruce Patton, Sheila Heen

Leadership without Easy Answers by Ronald A. Heifetz

Leading through Conflict by Mark Gerzon

Footnotes on Day 6
1 http://thinkexist.com/quotes

www.ingramcontent.com/pod-product-compliance
Lightning Source LLC
Chambersburg PA
CBHW020010050426
42450CB00005B/394